The Wackiest Nature Riddles on Earth

MIKE ARTELL

Sterling Publishing Co., Inc.   New York

To Steph and Joanna—
the Wackiest Daughters on Earth!
Love, Dad

Library of Congress Cataloging-in-Publication Data

Artell, Mike.
    The wackiest nature riddles on earth / written and illustrated by
Mike Artell.
      p.   cm.
    Includes index.
    Summary: Includes hundreds of riddles featuring ecological or
environmental topics, such as forests, mountains, birds, and
weather.
    ISBN 0-8069-1250-2
    1. Riddles, Juvenile.   2. Ecology—Juvenile humor.   3. Wit and
humor, Juvenile. [1. Riddles.   2. Ecology—Wit and humor.]
I. Title.
PN6371.5.A77   1992
818'.5402—dc20   91-45773
                                     CIP
                                     AC

 This book has been printed
on recycled paper.

10 9 8 7 6 5 4 3 2

First paperback edition published in 1993 by
Sterling Publishing Company, Inc.
387 Park Avenue South, New York, N.Y. 10016
© 1992 by Mike Artell
Distributed in Canada by Sterling Publishing
% Canadian Manda Group, P.O. Box 920, Station U
Toronto, Ontario, Canada M8Z 5P9
Distributed in Great Britain and Europe by Cassell PLC
Villiers House, 41/47 Strand, London WC2N 5JE, England
Distributed in Australia by Capricorn Link Ltd.
P.O. Box 665, Lane Cove, NSW 2066
Manufactured in the United States of America
All rights reserved

Sterling ISBN 0-8069-1250-2 Trade
            0-8069-1251-0 Paper

Contents

— 1 —
Ecolo-jests

What do ecologists eat for dessert?
Environ-mints.

What kind of stink do ecologists hate the most?
Ex-stink.

Why did the ecologist stay in front of the auk?
Because it was a tough auk (act) to follow.

What kind of tea do park rangers like to drink?
Yosemi-tea.

Anyone for Tea?

What kind of tea . . .

pulls everything towards the center of the earth?
Gravi-tea.

describes people or animals that live together?
Communi-tea.

creates thunder and lightning?
Electrici-tea.

describes things people own?
Proper-tea.

rules other people?
Royal-tea.

describes what you can do?
Abili-tea.

Where do ecologists get their mail?
At the com-post office.

What happened to the ecologist's biology grade when he didn't study?
It started to bio-degrade.

What did the ecologist say when he saw the skunk?
I wouldn't touch that thing with a ten-foot polecat!

Why did the sad ecologist write a poem about a rose?
Things went from bud to verse (bad to worse).

What did the ecologist do when her cat stayed out in the cold too long?
I think she thawed a puddy tat!

How did the ecologist feel about the trees that had turned to stone?
He was petrified!

What kind of wars do ecologists like best?
Reserv-wars (reservoirs).

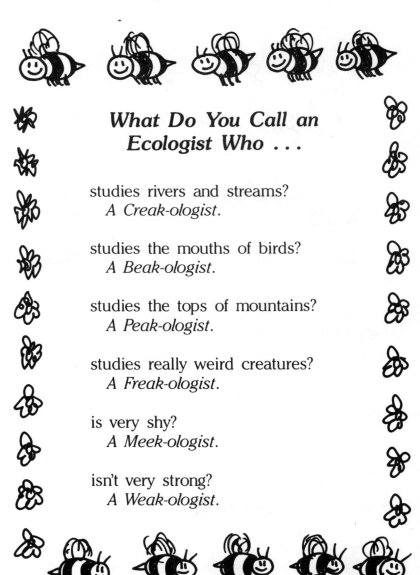

What Do You Call an Ecologist Who . . .

studies rivers and streams?
A Creak-ologist.

studies the mouths of birds?
A Beak-ologist.

studies the tops of mountains?
A Peak-ologist.

studies really weird creatures?
A Freak-ologist.

is very shy?
A Meek-ologist.

isn't very strong?
A Weak-ologist.

What kind of cakes do ecologists eat on their birthdays?

Ozone Layer Cakes.

What Is It?

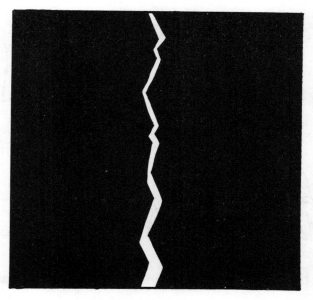

View of the world from inside an egg about to crack open

— 2 —
The Ocean

Who helped the beautiful fish go to the underwater ball?
Her fairy cod-mother.

What did the shellfish say when he heard he might be eaten?
Abalone!

Why was the sea urchin worried?
It didn't know if its neighbor was a friend or anemone (an enemy).

What kind of tea do sea mammals like to drink?
Mana-tee.

Which Ocean Creatures . . .

have the worst tempers?
The crabby ones.

are the quietest?
Those that clam up.

are the smallest?
The shrimps.

cry the most?
The whales.

are the most famous?
The starfish.

NO THANKS,
I JUST ATE!

What kind of vehicles do fish like to drive?
Bara-scooters (Barracudas).

What is the best kind
of can to catch fish in?
  A peli-can (pelican).

What's the one thing that keeps oceans from drying up?
  The water.

What kind of tide is always tearing things up?
  A rip tide.

Where do oceans like to show off and brag?
  Along the boast-line (coast line).

Which whale is the saddest?
  The blue whale.

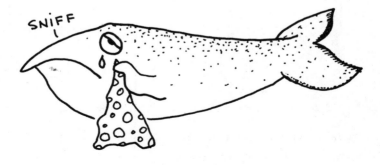

"I hope one day I'll meet a handsome Peanut Butter fish." Who am I?

A jellyfish.

"I hope one day I'll meet a beautiful nail head shark." Who am I?

A hammerhead shark.

What's a dolphin's favorite expression?

Sonar (so far)—so good.

What happens to electric eels after an earthquake?

They get aftershocks.

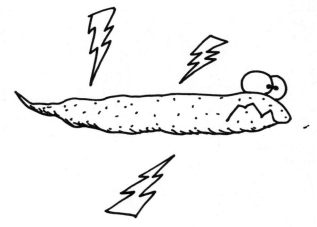

What kind of fins do porpoises have?
Dolph-fins (Dolphins).

Why is it hard to win any kind of game in the ocean?
Because the score is always tide (tied).

What kind of trees grow near the ocean?
Beach (Beech) trees.

What did the two whales say when they backed into each other?
All's whale that ends whale.

What kind of Mexican food does coral like?
Reef-fried (refried) beans.

How did the shark feel about the skeleton?
It made no bones about it.

What book
about the sea
is the wettest?
  *"20,000 Leaks (leagues)
  Under the Sea."*

What sea has the softest bottom?
The Muddy-terranean (Mediterranean).

What kind of crabs are the best salesmen?
The soft-sell crabs.

Why didn't the little crab bathe in the ocean?
It decided to wash up on shore instead.

Who visits all the good little lobsters on Christmas Eve?
Sandy Claws!

Where do sea cows sleep at night?
In barn-acles.

In what kind of water do people get most offensive?
In-sult water (in salt water).

What do you call sick oceans?
Dis-seas (disease).

Why should you always say "hello" to an ocean?
Because it will always wave back.

How did the whale explain its unusually large tail?
The whale said it was a fluke.

What do you call a blowfish that feels sorry for itself?
A whiny spiny in the briny.

What kind of jungle cats live near the ocean?
The coast-lions (coastlines).

Why was the oyster mad at the clam?
The clam was being shellfish.

What sign did they put on the seaweed buffet?
"KELP YOURSELF."

Why should you never bring good dishes to the beach?
Because the breakers are there.

What happened to the shrimp who lifted weights?
It got big mussels (muscles).

What kind of whale likes to barbecue?
  The griller whale.

What kind of whale likes to play jokes on other whales?
  The kidder (killer) whale.

What do little whales learn in school?
  Their A, B, Seas.

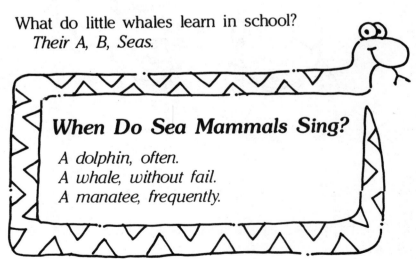

When Do Sea Mammals Sing?

A dolphin, often.
A whale, without fail.
A manatee, frequently.

Where do great white sharks keep their snacks?
In cookie Jaws.

When an ocean reads a book, what page does it read first?
The tidal (title) page.

What did the drop of oil say as it fell on the ocean?
"Oil sea you later."

3
Water, Water Everywhere

Where do rivers run when they hit a baseball?
To first basin (base).

Why didn't the lake like the pond?
The lake thought the pond was very shallow.

What did the spawning salmon tell its mate?
"See you next year—same time, same 'channel.'"

What kind of can holds the most water?
A can-al (canal).

What body of water is the easiest to hear?
The sound.

When is the best time to see a river flowing?
Current-ly.

How does a white-water canoeist paddle?
Rapid-ly.

Why did the dog want to get out of the canoe?
Because he was up the creek without a poodle.

Who is the Mississippi River married to?
Mr. Sippi.

What kind of news do rivers like best?
"Current" events.

How does a river see where it is going at night?
It uses a floodlight.

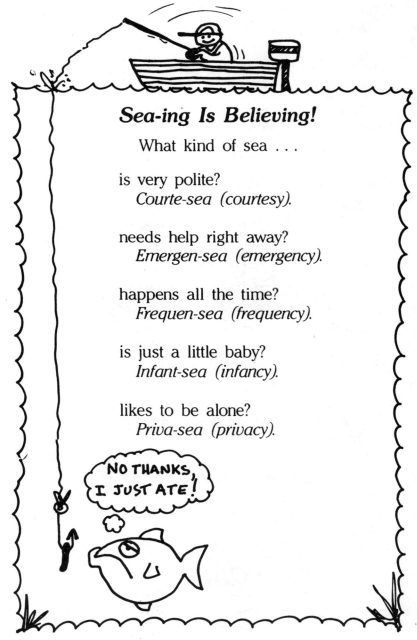

Sea-ing Is Believing!

What kind of sea . . .

is very polite?
Courte-sea (courtesy).

needs help right away?
Emergen-sea (emergency).

happens all the time?
Frequen-sea (frequency).

is just a little baby?
Infant-sea (infancy).

likes to be alone?
Priva-sea (privacy).

NO THANKS, I JUST ATE!

What are the noisiest bodies of water?
The creaks (creeks).

How do bodies of water say goodbye in Italy?
"A-river-derci."

Why is it impossible to die of thirst?
Because a small river is always "by you" (bayou).

What is the favorite food of wetland animals?
Marsh-mallows.

Why did the waterfowl leave the polluted lake?
It found the water foul.

Letters and Numbers

What three letters spell a certain kind of force?

N-R-G (energy).

What number and letter spell a place where trees grow?

4-S (forest).

What two letters spell a kind of seaweed?

L-J (algae).

What two letters spell a long, skinny fish?

E-L (eel).

What number and four letters spell an arm of the sea?

S-2-A-R-E (estuary).

4
Forests and Jungles

Why was the decaying tree so lucky?
It was in the rot place at the rot time.

What president do plants and trees like best?
Bush.

How are trees and dogs alike?
They both have a bark.

How are trees and rivers like your library system?
They all have branches.

How do rain forest animals feel about all the rain?
The monsoon-er, the better!

Crazy-Eights

What kind of eight . . .

do farmers like best?
Cultiv-8.

do farmers need to water their crops?
Irrig-8.

do people do when they talk?
Communic-8.

do people do when they work together?
Co-oper-8.

happens to animals that move around a lot?
Migr-8.

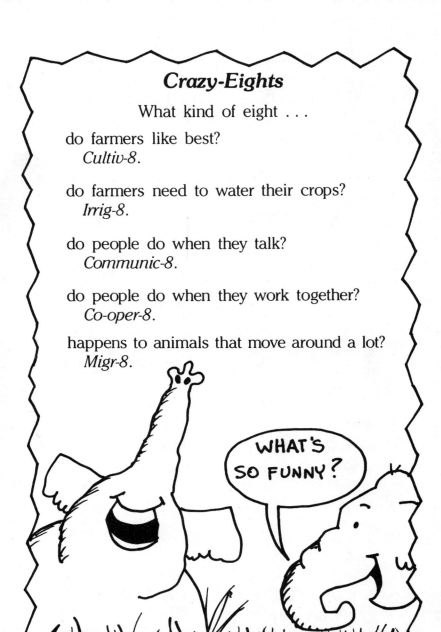

WHAT'S SO FUNNY?

Crazy-Eights

What kind of eight . . .

happens to water when you heat it?
Evapor-8.

happens to a seed when it sprouts?
Germin-8.

belongs to a creature with no backbone?
Invertebr-8.

is a chimpanzee?
Prime-8.

do bears like best?
Hibern-8.

WHAT'S SO FUNNY?

What kind of tree is always ready to shake hands?

The palm tree.

Why did the rotting tree start erasing all its music?

It was de-composing.

Why didn't the other trees hang around the maple tree?

The maple tree was a real sap.

After swimming in a polluted stream, the elephant developed a rash on its stomach. What did the vet tell him he had?

A toxic waist (waste).

Did the vet have any other bad news for the elephant?

Yes—the elephant also had poison ivory.

Why don't elephants wear sport coats?

Because they can't find the ELE-PANTS to match.

What did the boy ape say to the girl ape?
You're the gorilla (girl of) my dreams.

Where do South American llamas like to swim?
In the LLamazon River.

What do cobras hang in the bathroom?
Hiss and hers towels.

What is the toughest bat of all?
The baseball bat.

What do Australian marsupials like to drink?
Coca-Koala.

What's the favorite Christmas song in the rain forest?
"Jungle Bells."

The Worst That Can Happen

What's the worst thing that can happen to . . .

a giraffe?
A sore throat.

a shark?
Cavities.

an elephant?
A stuffy nose.

a centipede?
Sore feet.

an owl?
Losing a contact lens.

a snake?
Biting its tongue.

a honeybee?
Its mother won't let it eat sweets.

a kangaroo?
Getting trapped in a room with low ceilings.

WHEW!

Why are rain forest animals always so clean?
They take a lot of showers.

What kind of gulls live near the rain forests?
Jun-gulls (jungles).

The bear touched some toxic material. What did the vet tell him he had?
Paw-lution.

What Is It?

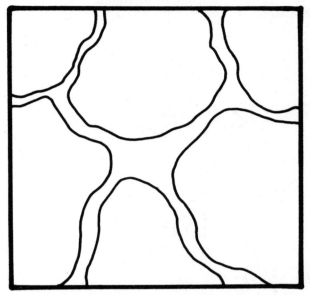

Close-up of a giraffe's neck

What is a jungle
cat's favorite
TV show?
   Leopardy.

Why was the king of the beasts worried about the weather?

Because there was only a 10% chance of its reigning.

Where do the smartest parrots live?

In the tropical BRAIN forest.

$E=MC^2$

5
The Desert

Who's got the most boring job in the desert?
The weatherman.

What kind of cartoons do they watch in the desert?
"Duney Tunes."

What canyon do older people like the most?
The Granny Canyon.

What do deserts say when they meet each other?
They say, "How you dune?"

What subject do cacti like best?
Dry spell-ing.

What did one rock say to the other at the rock party?
"Shale we dance?"

Where do toads jump the most?
  In the Mo-Hoppy (Mohave) Desert.

How do you get across a dry, arid grassland?
  Steppe by steppe.

What nursery rhyme do camels like best?
  The one about HUMP-ty Dumpty.

How do camels hide in the desert?
They wear camel-flage.

What did the dried-up lake bed say when it started raining?
Better lake than never.

What kind of stone is the most sour?
Lime-stone.

Why don't desert animals laugh much?
They have a very dry sense of humor.

What body of water in the desert never gets close to you?
The away-sis (oasis).

What kind of bird nests
do you find in the desert?
   Wilder-nests.

What's another name
for a sandstorm?
   A dust guster.

Why did the sandstorm
stop blowing?
   It was dis-gusted.

Where do jack rabbits live?
   In rabbit-tats (habitats).

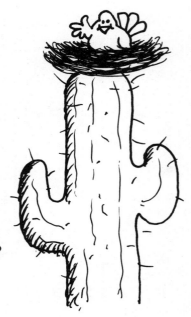

What did they sing at the jack rabbit reunion?
   "Hail, Hail, the gang's all EAR."

What's special about leaving your ice cream in Death Valley?
You desert your dessert in the desert.

What sign did they put up in Death Valley?
DUNE NOT ENTER.

6
Mountains and Volcanoes

Why was the mother volcano angry at her child?
Because it kept inter-erupting (interrupting).

What kind of hangers do mountains use in their closets?
Cliff-hangers.

How did everyone know the volcano was angry?
Because it was fuming.

What happened to the sea bird when she moved between two mountains?
She became a valley gull (girl).

What mountain range grows the most apples?
The Apple-lachian (Appalachian) Mountains.

What's the best way to describe a beautiful canyon?
Gorge-geous (gorgeous).

Where do mountains
cook their food?
On mountain ranges.

Why didn't the mountain believe the cliff?
It thought the cliff was bluff-ing.

What do mountain sheep eat each day at noon?
Ava-lunch (avalanche).

Who invented volcanoes and geysers?
Mr. Geo. Thermal.

What kind of music do most mountains like best?
Rock music.

What kind of music do the tallest mountains like?
Alti-tunes (altitudes).

Where do volcanoes
go to kiss?
Lava's lane.

─── 7 ───
Cold Places

Who brings Christmas presents to the baby moose?
 Antler-Claus.

What sounds cold, but can really keep you warm?
 Coal.

What do sea mammals put on their floors?
 Walrus to walrus (wall-to-wall) carpeting.

Two penguins were sitting on an ice floe. One
jumped into the water. What did the other one do?
 He decided to go with the floe (flow).

What animals were the absolute coolest?
 The ones from the Ice Age.

Why was the polar bear upset with her test grades?
They were all 20 below zero!

What kind of hairdo do most polar bears have?
A perm-a-frost.

What do lady polar bears put on their faces at night?
Very cold cream.

Where do we get the money to clean up melted snow?
From a slush fund.

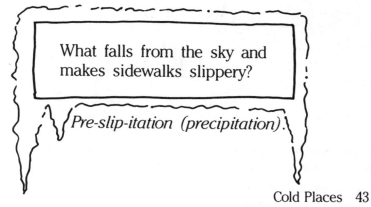

What falls from the sky and makes sidewalks slippery?

Pre-slip-itation (precipitation).

What are the friendliest things in the Arctic?
  Nicebergs.

What kind of cars do they drive at the South Pole?
  Antarcti-cars.

Where do you find the coldest ants?
  In Ant-arctica.

What country do bears go to in the winter?
  The hiber-nation.

What do penguins wear
to keep their heads warm?
   Polar ice caps.

What will you see on
penguins' faces when
they hear these jokes?
   Pen-grins.

What sound do cows
in the Arctic make?
   Eski-mooooo.

The polar bear used hair curlers that were powered
by the sun. What did she call them?
   Solar polar rollers.

How do they say "goodbye" at the North Pole?
   With a cold wave.

What do they shout when they cut trees in Alaska?
   Tim-brrrrr!

8
Down to Earth

What part of the earth is the scariest?
The EEEK-quator (equator).

What is the most selfish way of looking for ore?
MINE-ing (mining).

How is the earth like a piece of bread?
They both have a crust.

What is the favorite singing group of planet Earth?
The Four Seasons.

What kind of toe is the flattest?

A plat-toe (plateau).

Why did everyone trust the plateau?
Because they knew it was on the level.

What happened to the very bad plateau?
His parents grounded him.

Why was the continent so misunderstood?
Because no one could get its "drift."

Where do continents put their plates when they're through eating?
On the Continental Shelf.

Where is the best spot
on earth to see things?
On an EYE-land (island).

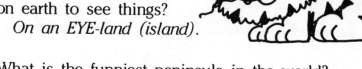

What is the funniest peninsula in the world?
Ba-Ha-Ha-Ha California (Baja California).

What kind of natural disaster are ducks most afraid of?
Earth-quacks.

What is the favorite drink of polar earthquakes?
Frozen shakes.

What kind of sand is always in a hurry?
Quicksand.

Naturally Polite

What does a polite snake say after it bites you?
"Fang you very much."

What does a polite plant say to a farmer?
"Thank you very mulch."

What do polite sheep say to each other?
"Thank ewe very much."

What do polite kittens say to each other?
"Thank you furry much."

THAT'S HILL-LARIOUS!

How on Earth?

How does . . .

a lost hunter walk around?
Aim-lessly.

a gorilla eat a banana?
A-peel-ingly.

a frightened calf act?
Cow-wardly.

a canine animal pursue its prey?
Dog-gedly.

a geyser express its feelings?
Gush-ingly.

a hyena tell its story?
Laugh-ingly.

a duck do its work?
Pro-duck-tively.

a leopard clean its house?
Spot-lessly.

a woodpecker peck a tree?
Hole-somely.

WHEW!

9
Down on the Farm

What piece of land is always in pain?
An acre.

Why did the gopher move out of its hole in the farmer's garden?
The gopher didn't "dig" it anymore.

Why was the farmer
getting bored with
the musical garden tool?
It was a "Hoe-hummm."

Why are farmers so smart?
Because they "weed" (read) a lot.

How do really weird farmers water their crops?
They use eerie-gation (irrigation).

Why did the farmer buy so much land?
He got it "dirt" cheap.

Why didn't anybody like the dirty porcupine?
Because he was a stick in the mud.

What do you call a porcupine that doesn't feel well?
A sicker sticker.

Why are chickens the poorest farm animal?
Because they can never make "hens" meet (make ends meet).

Why do chickens make good ecologists?
Because they're concerned about the Henvironment.

Who was the meanest chicken that ever lived?
Attila the Hen.

What sound did the rooster make while he was cooking dinner?
"Cock-a-Noodle-Stew!"

What do cows shout when they're surfing?
"Cow-abunga!!"

What do cows shout when they jump out of airplanes?
   "Geronimoooo!"

What do you call a cow that plays the violin?
   "Fiddler on the Hoof."

Where do most cows go for sun and fun?
   Cow-lifornia.

Why do cows like school so much?
   They always get good graze (grades).

What's the difference between a car that uses too much gas and a cow?
   One is a gas guzzler and the other is a grass guzzler.

Where do pigs go for sun and fun?
   To the National Porks.

What kind of pigs live near the equator?
   The Tro-pigs.

What kind of topsoil do pigs like best?
  Slop-soil.

What political office did the lady horse run for?
  Mare (Mayor).

What kind of pollution hurts foxes the most?
  Foxic waste.

What Is It?

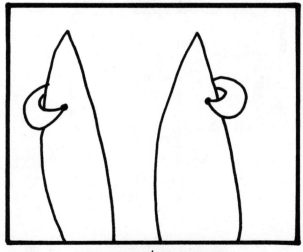

Rabbit with pierced ears

The Very Best

What do electric eels do best?
Shock.

What do monkeys do best?
Mock.

What do birds of a feather do best?
Flock.

What do woodpeckers do best?
Knock.

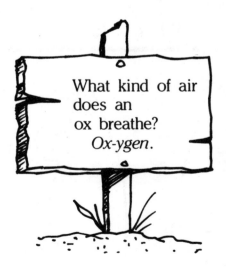

What kind of air
does an
ox breathe?
Ox-ygen.

— 10 —
Strictly for the Birds

What endangered animal never uses a comb?
The bald eagle.

What would you call an eagle who could play the piano with its feet?
Very TALON-ted.

Why do eagles go to church?
Because they're birds of pray (prey).

Which birds drink the most?
The swallows.

Why did the tropical bird hang around with the cocker spaniel?
The bird was a cockatoo (cocker too).

Where do birds go
when they're sick?
To see the duck-tor.

What kind of bird
has the weirdest haircut?
The mo-hawk.

What sound does a bird's telephone make?
Wing! Wing!

What kind of birds like to play with Hula Hoops?
Hooping (whooping) cranes.

What kind of birds
do bees like most?
Buzzz-ards.

How did the ugly duckling
feel when she grew up?
Swan-derful!

What kind of birds can't fly and make really bad jokes?
Pun-guins.

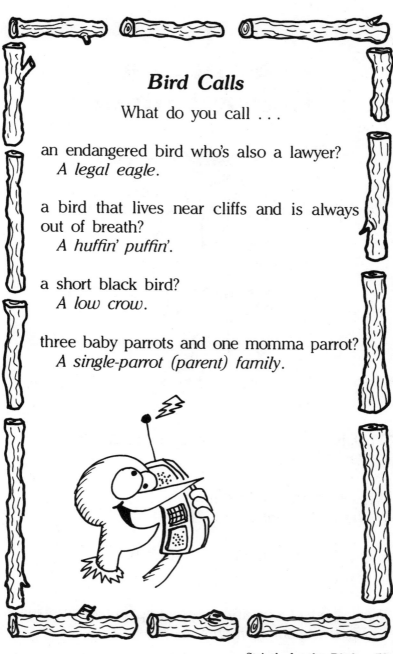

Bird Calls

What do you call . . .

an endangered bird who's also a lawyer?
  A legal eagle.

a bird that lives near cliffs and is always out of breath?
  A huffin' puffin'.

a short black bird?
  A low crow.

three baby parrots and one momma parrot?
  A single-parrot (parent) family.

— 11 —
Ants, Bugs and Creepy Critters

What is Arnold Schwarzenegger's favorite bug?
The Germinator.

What kind of ants are the worst?
The Pollute-ants.

What kind of ants are almost as bad?
Contamin-ants.

What kind of contamin-ants jump out of airplanes?
Airborne contamin-ants.

What kind of bugs hang around bowling alleys?
Bowl weevils.

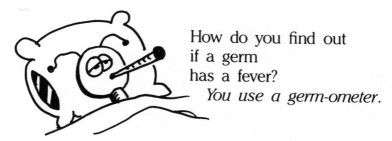

How do you find out
if a germ
has a fever?
    You use a germ-ometer.

What kind of cars do bugs in the wetlands drive?
Swamp buggies.

What do you call a colony of ants at the North Pole?
A COOL-ony of ants.

What would you call it if worms took over the world?
Global worming.

What do bees use to make their hair look nice?
Honey combs.

What do you call
a coffee cup
for an insect?
  A bug mug.

What two ticks did Noah round up?
  Arc-ticks.

What do you call a Click Beetle that has put on weight?
  A thicker clicker.

What do butterflies sleep on?
  Cater-pillows.

When ants run away to get married, what deers help them?

Ant-elopes.

What happens when you use bug spray?

Bugs pray.

What side of the Lawn and Garden store do bugs hate the most?

The pesti-side (pesticide).

12
Something's Fishy

Why did the fish decide to paint a picture instead of eat dinner?

Because one picture is worth a thousand worms (words).

Who do fish call when they want a pizza?

Dom-Minnows Pizza (Domino's).

What do fish do when they're bored?

They read a good brook (book).

Where do fish keep their garden tools?
In watersheds.

Where do fish put dishes that don't float?
In the sink.

What kind of fruit do fish like best?
Watermelon.

How did the mother fish know the little fish had done something wrong?
It had a gill-ty (guilty) look.

How do fish weigh themselves?
On their scales.

Where do fish learn to swim?
In schools.

What singers do fish like the best?
Salmon (Simon) and Garfunkel.

What fish get
along best?
*Sole (soul)
mates.*

What sport do fish like best?
Bass-ketball.

What fish do you call in to fix your piano?
A tuna (tuner).

What do fish get if they don't like the bait
that fishermen are using?
They get a re-bait (rebate).

13
Reptiles and Amphibians

What kind of reptiles are the best farmers?
The fertiliz-ards.

Who helped the little girl reptile get back to Kansas?
The Lizard of Oz.

What do alligators use to wake up every day?
Clock-odiles.

How did the mother snake keep the baby snake happy?
She gave him his own rattle.

What Is It?

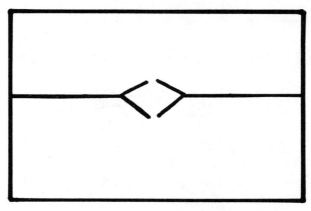

*Close-up of two snakes sticking their
tongues out at each other*

What kind of shoes do snakes wear for swimming?
Water moccasins.

Why don't snakes eat cacti?
They think it tastes YUCCA!

Which reptiles have the best memories?
The ones with turtle (total) recall.

What do you call an amphibian in a mist?
A fog frog.

What soft drink do frogs like best?
Croaker-Cola.

What kind of aunts do frogs have?
Aunt-phibians.

What kind of animals like "rap" music?
Rap-tiles.

What kind of frogs tell the most lies?
Am-fib-ians.

Where do the coldest frogs live?
At the tad-POLES.

Why do frogs eat flies?
They like "fast" food.

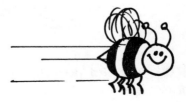

14
Environ-Mentals

If a plant were elected president, where would it live?

In the Green House.

How do jungle cats talk to each other?

Over the telephone lion.

What happens when pandas get out of control?

Panda-monium.

What singer do monkeys like the most?

Debbie Baboon.

What kind of job did the little otter get?
A job as a short "otter" cook.

How did he do as a short "otter" cook?
He was an "otter" failure.

Why are deer always willing to lend you money?
*Because even when they don't have a lot of "doe,"
they always have at least one "buck."*

What's the scariest deer of all?
The cari-boo!

How many mice can a hungry owl eat?
Owl of them.

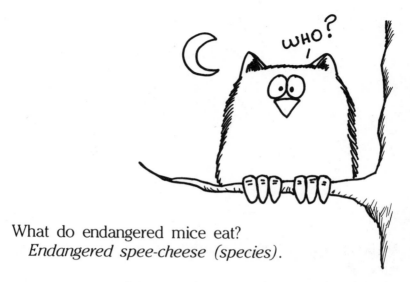

What do endangered mice eat?
Endangered spee-cheese (species).

Why did they throw the mouse into the oil slick?
To stop it from squeaking.

What did the mother mouse tell the little mouse?
Don't squeak until you're spoken to.

What kind of dent did the mouse put into the canoe?
A row-dent (rodent).

What do you call tennis shoes for mice?
Squeaker sneakers.

What family of small animals is the worst to have around?
The verte-brats.

What animal did Noah like best?
Noah's Auk.

Why was the momma kangaroo so happy with her little baby?
Because she knew it was "in the bag."

What long period of time sounds like a mistake?
An era (error).

What kind of map of the earth is the most calm?
A relief map.

What animal is the most selfish?
The gimme-pig (guinea pig).

You Make the Call

What do you call . . .

a conversation between two birds of prey?
Hawk talk.

a letter sent to Moby Dick?
Whale mail.

the king of the jungle getting a tan on the beach?
A fryin' lion.

something a bunny does without thinking?
A rabbit habit.

an honest-to-goodness sea lion?
A real seal.

a python made out of rubber?
A fake snake.

What is the greatest fear of all?
The atmos-fear (atmosphere).

What kind of doll do little girl bears play with?
Bearbie (Barbie) Dolls.

What do you call a bear that got caught in the rain?
A drizzly bear.

What organization did the little bear want to join?
The Cub Scouts.

What singing group do animals like the best?
The Gnu Kids on the Block.

Where do fairy-tale characters put their trash?
In the Humpty Dump.

What is a giraffe's favorite drink?
Neck-tar.

Where do zebras go for sun and fun?
To the zee-shore.

— 15 —
Big Breezes
and More About
the Weather

What do they call a strong breeze in the South?
A squall, you all.

What are the craziest kinds of tornadoes?
Psycho-clones (cyclones).

What do you get if you make
an exact copy of a cyclone?
A cyclone-clone.

Why did the cyclone keep
coming back?
Because it was a recycl-one.

What Do You Call the Air ...

around a flying mammal?
The bat-mosphere.

around a feline?
The cat-mosphere.

around small biting insects?
The gnat-mosphere.

around a rodent?
The rat-mosphere?
Nope ...  *the at-mouse-sphere.*

What Kind of Warm Weather Do You Always Find . . .

near a rabbit?
A warm hare mass.

near some fungi?
A warm air moss.

underground?
A worm air mass.

WHAT'S SO FUNNY?

What kind of storm moves the fastest?
A hurry-cane (hurricane).

What movie do hurricanes like best?
"Gone With the Wind."

What book do hurricanes like best?
"The Squall (Call) of the Wild."

What's the grouchiest kind of wind?

A crosswind.

What nursery rhyme do baby thunderstorms like best?
"Sprinkle, Sprinkle, Little Star."

— 16 —
Toughies

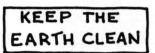

ECOLOGIST: You'll never get a tan by staying under-water.

FISHERMAN: I didn't say I wanted a tan. I said I wanted to catch a few rays.

What did the ecologist yell when he felt the earth quake?

"Turf's up!"

How did the polluting pirates kill the krill?

They made it walk the plankton.

What kind of tree always feels sad?
The sigh-press (cypress).

_SIGH!

ECOLOGIST #1: That earthquake was terrible. It made a huge crack in the ground!
ECOLOGIST #2: Well, don't yell at me! It's not my "fault"!

Where do ecologists go fishing?
In the John J. Audu-pond (Audubon).

ECOLOGIST #1: Who won the election in Erosion City?
ECOLOGIST #2: No one yet . . . they're having a run-off.

Where do elands (antelopes) throw their garbage?
In eland-fill.

When two monkeys get married, what do they become?
Primates.

Why did the little flat-topped mountain get punished?
Because it made a mesa (mess of) its room.

What did one rock say when it made friends with another rock?
"I've taken a lichen (a liking) to you."

What kind of violin did the talented mountain play?
A strata-varius (Stradivarius).

What kind of bad weather do they have near the Arctic Circle?
Tundra-storms (thunderstorms).

Would you rather live up in the clouds or underground?
I don't know—it's an "ether/ore" (either/or) decision.

THERE'S NO PLACE
LIKE BIOME

Which bird spends the most?
I'm not sure, but every toucan has a big bill.

What book do skunks like best?
"The Power of Positive Stinking."

What kind of camel has the most rhythm?
The drummer-dary (dromedary).

Why wasn't the sea bird
sorry for what it did?
Because it had no "egrets."

What kind of oil
has the worst manners?
Crude oil.

What kind of rocks are never trusted by other rocks?
The kind that gyps-'em (gypsum).

Why was the farmer arrested for cooking eggs?
There are laws against poaching.

It's Hard to Describe . . .

How would you describe two whales fighting over some suntan oil?
An ocean lotion commotion.

How would you describe a lion, a fox, a timid mouse and a desert lizard?
His Highness, His Slyness, His Shyness and His Dryness.

How would you describe an unusual female horse jumping on a trampoline?
A rare mare in mid-air.

How would you describe a beaver, a frog, a pig and a big fish?
A chopper, a hopper, a slopper and a whopper.

What kind of disposable diapers do South American ecologists put on their babies?
Pampas.

It's Hard to Describe ...

How would you describe an artistic tropical bird with a broken wing?
A macaw with a flaw that can draw with its claw.

How would you describe some baby pigs, a mother hen on her eggs, a singing bird and a grandma?
A litter, a sitter, a twitter and a knitter.

How would you describe the world's biggest ocean, some Egyptian drawings and a perfectly clean environment?
Pacific, hieroglyphic and terrific!

What Is It?

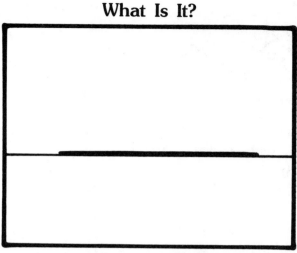

Sea-level view of an oil slick

What pirate are most fish afraid of?
Captain Hook.

Hi, Sis!

What kind of "sis" . . .

brings water to the desert?
Oa-sis.

turns sunlight into plant food?
Photosynthe-sis.

turns a caterpillar into a butterfly?
Metamorpho-sis.

WHEW!

How did all the animals know the water wasn't polluted anymore?

The sign near the hole said, "Well Water."

What does everyone in Panama shout on December 25th?

"Merry Isthmus!"

Glossary

Abalone . . . . A large sea snail
Aftershock . . . . A small earthquake that follows a large earthquake
Altitude . . . . How high something is above the earth or water
Amphibians . . . . Animals such as frogs that live on land and water
Anemone . . . . An underwater creature with tentacles that looks like a flower
John J. Audubon . . . . . . A famous American painter and naturalist
Auk . . . . A sea bird that lives along northern sea coasts
Basin . . . . The low land that a river drains into
Bayou . . . . A small stream that flows through a swamp or marsh
Biodegrade . . . . To decay or break down and return to the environment
Biome . . . . A group of living things in a specific region or area
Compost . . . . Fertilizer made mostly of decayed materials
Contaminants . . . . Things that pollute or infect other things
Continental Shelf . . . . . . An underwater plain that forms the edge of a continent
Crosswind . . . . A wind that blows sideways across a person or thing
Cyclone . . . . A windy storm that spins in a very fast circle
Decomposing . . . . Breaking down or decaying into its most basic parts
Ecologist . . . . A scientist who studies living things and their environments
Egret . . . . A large bird with long, thin legs and large feathers on the top of its head
Eland . . . . A kind of African antelope
Endangered species . . . Living things that are dangerously close to extinction

Ether . . . . The outer edge of the earth's atmosphere

Fault . . . . A crack in the outside layer of the earth

Floe . . . . A flat piece of floating ice

Fluke . . . . The flat, triangular fin on a whale's tail

Geothermal . . . . Having to do with the heat inside the earth

Global warming . . . . The idea that the earth may be getting warmer

Gnu . . . . An African antelope with horns and a head like an ox

Gypsum . . . . A white, chalky mineral

Habitat . . . . The place where plants or animals live and grow

Irrigation . . . . A man-made way of bringing water to dry areas

Isthmus . . . . A skinny piece of land connecting two larger bodies of land

Kelp . . . . A kind of seaweed

Lichen . . . . A simple plant that grows on rocks and trees

Marsupials . . . . Mammals that keep their young in their pouches

Metamorphosis . . . . The change a thing or creature goes through to become a different kind of thing or creature

Mojave Desert . . . . A desert in southern California

Monsoon . . . . The rainy season in Southeast Asia and India

Oil slick . . . . A thin film of oil on the surface of water

Ozone layer . . . . The area of the earth's atmosphere 20–30 miles up

Pampas . . . . A grassy, South American plain

Peninsula . . . . A body of land surrounded on three sides by water

Precipitation . . . . Water or ice in the atmosphere that falls to earth in the form of rain, snow, sleet or hail

Permafrost . . . . Land that is permanently frozen

Photosynthesis . . . . The way plants turn sunlight and water into food

Plankton . . . . Tiny, floating plants and animals that make up the basic food supply in the ocean

Plateau . . . . Flat, level land that is higher than surrounding land

Polar ice caps . . . . Giant sheets of ice that cover both poles

Relief map . . . . A map with bumpy, raised areas for mountains and flat, smooth areas for water

Reptiles . . . . Snakes, turtles, alligators and other air-breathing creatures with scales

Run-off . . . . Water that is not collected and flows down the sides of hills and other bodies of land

Sedimental . . . . Anything that deals with material that sinks to the bottom of a liquid

Shale . . . . Rock that easily splits into layers

Sonar . . . . An electronic device that can locate things underwater by using sound waves

Squall . . . . A storm with strong gusts of wind

Steppe . . . . A dry, grassy plain that gets both very hot and very cold

Strata . . . . Layers of earth

Toxic waste . . . . Anything that is thrown away and can harm living things

Tundra . . . . A plain without trees that is usually very cold

Turf . . . . Grassy soil

Watershed . . . . The area that a body of water drains into

Yucca . . . . A desert plant that has white flowers

About the Author

Mike Artell is the author and illustrator of dozens of children's picture books and activity books. He has also created scores of greeting cards and many, many cartoons for national magazines. For two years, he also taught children how to write and draw cartoons on his Saturday-morning television show, and he visits with thousands of children at dozens of schools each year.

Mike lives in Mandeville, Louisiana, with his wife, Susan, his daughters, Stephanie and Joanna, and their cat, Tabu.

Index